Faith allows the Eyes of the Heart to See

Acknowledgments

I could not be blessed with a more genuine, spiritual and supportive mother. My Momma, Dr. Sybil Burgess-Murray, inspires me in everything she does and everything she is. There are no words to express how thankful I feel to have such an amazing Mother.

My Father, Lindsay Miller III, has always provided me with a stellar example of what it means to be a "good Daddy." His unconditional love has given me the strength to be the person I am today. He and my Step-Mother, Judy, were a huge help in getting my Mustang adventures "Jump-started." They have BOTH truly been assets in this amazing journey!

My sister, Mikaela Anderson, has been a huge help editing this book. Her love and support is invaluable - with respect to the book as well as life in general. Dirt is way thicker than blood.

Barbara Arntsen, author, entrepreneur and my Mom #2 has offered me brilliant insight. She has a way of cultivating new ideas within me - ideas that might have otherwise faded away. Thinking "outside of the box" is where her mind sets up camp and I love to visit with her there.

My daughter, Filleigh Kay, is an inspiration daily with her honest spirit and adventurous heart. I pray to always blanket her with the same unconditional love and support that I have been blessed with. The overwhelming love I feel towards her makes me that much more appreciative of the love I have received from my parents over the years.

To every horse I have been blessed to have a relationship with, I thank you with all my heart; Cap, Nugget, Misty, Easy, Smash, Rox - and now Lindsay's Faith, as well as all the others - I simply would not be "me" without each of them. My teachers, my mentors, they are not only the catalyst to my dreams - they ARE my dreams, as well as my reality.

I owe everything I am to the horse.

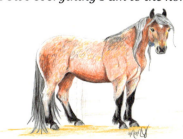

Dedication

I would like to dedicate this book to my husband, my best friend, J. Mike Jordan. I am forever grateful for his love and support of my extravagant dreams and aspirations.

Table of Contents

I. Life in the Wild

Freezing cold wind blew through the manes of the American Mustang herd in White Mountain, Wyoming. Wild mustang fillies Lenny, Jamie and Filleigh Kay kept warm by chasing one another around the scrub bushes, switching leads with each bounce and change of direction.

Soon the fillies rounded the last bush and took off at a full gallop, making a bee-line to Queen, Lenny's mother. The three foals slammed on brakes, skidding to a stop just before they reached the big bay mare. Queen looked at the playful fillies with interest and affection. It was part of her job to allow them freedom to play and grow while protecting them from danger.

1

Lenny's mother, Queen, was a striking mare. She was a bay, her hair coat fire red in color and her legs jet black. She had a small white star set between her eyes and her ears curved inward to a point at the tips. Her mane was unique, it was not black like that of a typical bay horse. It was bright silver and it danced in the sun.

Lenny stood beside Queen to catch her breath from her playful run. She gazed up at her mother's silver mane and dark brown eyes. She admired her so much. As a matter of fact, all the mustangs admired Lenny's mother.

Lenny's very own mother was the lead mare of the entire herd! This meant all of the horses, young and old, respected her and looked to her for guidance. She made every important decision for the herd - when to move on to the water hole, when to lay down to rest, when to run from danger. When any mustang walked by her, they politely moved out of her way.

Lenny adored how her mother's unique silver mane sparkled in the light of the sun and the moon. As Lenny gazed up, into her mother's deep brown eyes she said, "Momma, I want to be just like you when I grow up."

Queen's muzzle fluttered softly as she nickered and replied to her filly, "Lenny, you can be anything you want to be as long as you remember two things. You must always have Faith in yourself and you must also have Faith that there is something much more powerful than you, that has your best interest at heart. There is a unique path meant for your hooves only. The eyes of your heart are the only eyes that can see your path, and Faith allows those eyes to see."

A puzzled Lenny said, "So, my heart must grow eyes for me to be like you, Momma?"

Queen nickered a chuckle and replied, "You will see Lenny. In time you will see. You were named for the great herd sire 'Lindsay'. He was known for his deep Faith and he was a wonderful teacher of Faith to others. You just remember to have Faith and the eyes in your heart will take care of themselves."

Lenny thought to herself that it was no wonder her mother always seemed to know where she was - she had eyes growing out of all sorts of places! She thought hard about what her mother had said, but this word "Faith" she just simply could not understand.

She asked her mother, "What *is Faith*, Momma?"

Queen replied, "Faith is trust in the un-known. There is a path laid out special, for your hooves only. Faith allows your heart to see this path. Just believe that the path exists and that there is a power bigger than all of us who is taking care of us. Believe it, even though you can not see it. Believing is Faith."

Lenny took a deep sigh and felt her mother's silver mane brush her back as she stood close to her side, thinking about what it meant to have Faith.

II. The Gather

*T*he years went on and Lenny's mane grew long and silver, just like her mother's. Once Lenny grew up she left her mother's herd and joined a herd of her own. Living in the wild of White Mountain, Wyoming was not always easy, but Lenny had her herdmates and they gave her warmth, comfort and security.

Lenny grazed on the rough brush that grew from the ground for food. Some days Lenny's herd would travel many miles to find a good grazing spot. The winters were cold and Lenny would gather close to her herdmates to stay warm from the freezing wind.

Lenny's herd meant everything to her. The mustangs took comfort in each other. They constantly read one another's body language to communicate about food, water and safety.

One cold Wyoming day, something appeared in the sky that would change Lenny's life forever. It resembled a large black bird, but made a loud noise. It was a helicopter and it seemed bigger and louder by the second as it drew closer to Lenny's herd.

Lenny and the other mustangs let out a loud snort as they threw their heads high in the sky. In an instant, as if they were moving as one, the entire herd took off at a full gallop.

Lenny and her herdmates ran. They remained close together as they galloped across the rough terrain. They used their long legs and strong hooves to flee from the helicopter in the sky.

Lenny's herd galloped together, away from the helicopter. In the distance they spotted a lone horse. He was running at top speed and headed in the same direction as Lenny's herd. He appeared to know exactly where he was going, and this gave the mustangs security and guidance. So they continued to run, now following in the path of this lone horse.

The helicopter began to appear smaller in the sky as Lenny and her mustang herd followed behind the lone horse. They began to slow to a relaxed trot as the helicopter moved away. Then, as quickly as it had appeared, the helicopter was gone. The herd followed the lone horse into a group of bushes and then they all stopped.

Lenny looked around and much to her surprise, the bushes appeared to be connected together. They did not look like bushes she had ever seen before. They created a barrier that seemed to confine her, but she had the security of her herdmates and that gave her comfort.

On the other side of the bushes, Lenny spotted the lone horse standing calmly with his hind leg cocked in resting position. Lenny stepped towards him and said, "Hi there Mister, my name is Lenny. I sure hope you do not mind my asking, but what in the world is going on? My herd and I are a bit confused."

The lone horse replied, "No worries my dear, I do not mind near a bit. They call me 'PaPa' around here and I've helped numerous herds, just like yours, find their way into these pens made of bushes."

Lenny piped up, "Well, we were actually quite relieved to see you up ahead. You looked so confident, as if you knew exactly where we all should go. We were happy to follow. I still do not see why we are now in these pens made of bushes."

9

PaPa flicked an ear toward Lenny as he replied, "Well you see Lenny, fact is, there is only enough grass on these lands to feed some of the wild mustangs. There's not enough for every one of you which is why some mustangs must be gathered up. They are to be taken to a place where they'll be fed and cared for and others are left to live out in the wild."

Lenny could not quite follow what PaPa was trying to explain, but she sure appreciated the fact that he was so calm. Her mustang herd fed off the energy of other mustangs. After the adrenaline of the run, she was happy to rest quietly and PaPa sure helped her to rest.

Lenny said, "Well, thank you so much PaPa for trying to explain and thank you especially for giving me some guidance back there while my herd was running."

Papa nickered softly in approval as he dropped his head and let his eyes slowly close to rest.

III. New Surroundings

*M*orning came and Lenny and her herdmates were guided into a large box. Although unfamiliar, it was big and it seemed much quieter than the white bags making weird noises behind them, so she and her herdmates went inside. After a long ride from Wyoming, the box was opened at the Bureau of Land Management (BLM) holding facility in Colorado.

As Lenny peered out of the box, she could not believe her eyes! There were thousands of mustangs - so many more than her small herd from White Mountain. There were numerous piles of what appeared to be pulled-up grass and mustangs standing calmly, eating them. There were also large tubs filled with water. Lenny had never seen so much water. She was not sure what to think, it all seemed so foreign to her.

There were pipe rails that resembled trees to Lenny. They confined Lenny and her herd to that area, called a paddock. There were large piles of grass, called hay. Tubs of water were everywhere. Lenny wanted to taste the hay and she really wanted to drink the water, but she was afraid. She had never drank water from a tub before. She stood quietly and just watched the other mustangs to see what they did.

A strange-looking mustang approached Lenny. He had an odd growth coming out of his back, which made Lenny a bit fearful, so she took a few steps away as he approached.

He said, "Hello there. You must be a newbie. My name is Chief Horse, but they call me C.H. This growth you see on my back is one of the two-leggeds. I know he looks funny, but he's a good guy. He and I go around and make sure all of you are taken care of. We fill up your water tubs and bring you hay."

C.H. could see the puzzlement in Lenny's face, and he said, "Go ahead, take a drink of water. I know it looks funny in these tubs, but it's safe. See, I'll take a drink." C.H. then took a long drink of water from the tub.

C.H. said "I am a mustang like you, ya' know. I know you are afraid, but it will be ok. They feed us good here and if you're real lucky you might even get a forever home."

Lenny replied, "A forever home? What is that?"

C.H. answered, "Well it's kind of like here, but it's also like living in the wild. The best of both really. In a forever home you'll have your own two-legged, like I do. You'll explore new places together. It is much like the freedom we have in the wild, but with a two-legged as your herd-mate you will have feed and water in your tub every night."

Lenny dropped her head and took a long drink of water from the tub as C.H. had shown her. She began to day dream of a forever home.

IV. The Power of Words

*T*ime went on. The BLM facility where Lenny lived provided piles of hay every day and Lenny's water tub was always full. Lenny continued to dream of her forever home. One day as C.H. came to check on Lenny, he told her there was an adoption coming up. This might be Lenny's chance at a forever home!

The two-leggeds came and looked at Lenny and the other mustangs. Some mustangs were moved into the box and away to their forever homes. No one wanted Lenny, they said she was too old. More adoptions came and went. Lenny just grew older.

The other mustangs began to tease her. They said it was her funny-looking silver mane that no one wanted. Their words hurt Lenny so deeply. It was that very silver mane that had made her feel so close to her mother. She had adored her mother's silver mane. Now the very thing of which she had once felt so proud, she felt ashamed. Maybe it was her silver mane that no one wanted? Lenny felt so sad and so small.

Lenny hung her head low and stayed away from the herd. She was embarrassed by her silver mane. She wished that her mane was black or brown like the other mustangs.

Why did her mane have to be silver? It was not fair. She was mad, mad that her mane was silver, mad at her mother for giving her this ugly silver mane and mad at herself for not deserving a forever home.

Lenny was standing alone, quietly eating her pile of hay, when a newbie trotted up to her. He was a young mustang, coal black in color with a hint of white roaning over his flanks. He had recently been gathered up from the wild. When Lenny saw him looking, she quickly turned so the newbie mustang could not see her silver mane.

The mustang said boldly, "Hi, my name is Mikey. I could not help but come and tell you that I LOVE your silver mane. It is so unique and the sun makes it just sparkle - ohhhhhhh, you must be so very proud of it."

Lenny was so caught off guard by the compliment, she was not sure quite what to say. She finally managed to muster out a stuttered, "T-t-t-thank you, Mikey."

Mikey politely nodded his head in approval and spun around to trot off. Lenny just stood there, a bit in shock, as his words began to sink in. She thought about her silver mane, and as she did, she also began to think of her mother's words about Faith.

Have Faith, Lenny. Have Faith in yourself. Have Faith that there is something bigger than you, with your best interest at heart. Your Faith will open the eyes of your heart and you will then be able to see your special path - the path meant for your hooves only.

Lenny felt her eyes water as she played back her mother's words. As she repeated them over and over in her mind, she began to feel her spirits lift. It was as if she could actually feel herself growing taller and bigger inside.

The more she dwelt on her mother's words about Faith, the more the sadness that had engulfed her slowly dissipated. Her heart felt lighter and a welcomed sense of peace began to surround her.

The world around her even looked different. The mean mustangs that had seemed so large and daunting now seemed small and insignificant. Lenny no longer felt sad and ashamed.

She began to feel confident in herself, confident in her mother's words, confident in her Faith.

As she caught a glimpse of the silver mane cradling her face she could almost hear her mother's soft whicker of pride and approval.

V. Embrace Your Unique Qualities

*L*enny's paddock gate swung open wide as C.H. boldly entered and said, "I have exciting news! There is a new competition designed to help you older, unwanted mustangs find forever homes."

He then explained that this challenge was created by the Mustang Heritage Foundation and that he needed one hundred wild mustangs that were six years old.

Lenny's heart skipped a beat, she *was* six years old! Lenny knew this was her path. Her heart felt it. The strength she gained after Mikey's kind words had given her the confidence she needed for her heart to grow eyes to see.

C.H. said, "Now, it's gonna' take more than just a date of birth to get you into this deal. They are looking for mustangs with exceptional physical and mental strength. These one hundred mustangs will represent all mustangs to the world. If you have a unique trait that will set you apart from the rest, now is the time to let us know. These two-leggeds want to see the diversity of the mustang. If you have something special to offer, then let's see it now!"

Lenny's first thought went to her silver mane. It was unique, no doubt about that. She had grown so used to hiding it from the others, that even with her newfound inspiration from Mikey's comments and her recollection of her mother's words, she still struggled with what to do.

The two-leggeds stood outside of Lenny's paddock. They scribbled on their note-pads and studied the mustangs. There was a huge herd between Lenny and the two-leggeds. As Lenny tried to find her courage and move through the herd to reach the front, one of the mustangs taunted,"You better not let them see that ugly silver mane! No way they'll pick you if they see that thing."

Lenny began to sink back in shame and turn around. Then she stopped and re-minded herself, "No, I will *NOT* let their negative words control *my* path, I will have Faith - I *DO* have Faith." With that thought, she shook her head and tossed away the negative words.

As she shook her head, her long silver mane bounced up high in the air, high above the large herd of mustangs. In that same moment in time, one of the two-leggeds caught a glimmer of light out of the corner of his eye. He turned his head and spotted Lenny in the back of the herd.

The two-legged proclaimed, "Hey, let's pick that one there in the back with that unique silver mane. What a neat looking mustang that one is." Then he scribbled something down on his pad.

VI. On My Path

*L*enny was herded into the big box, along with the other mustangs selected for the challenge. After a long ride from Colorado, they were put in paddocks at the Piney Woods BLM facility near Jackson, Mississippi.

The two-leggeds brought them new piles of hay and filled their tubs with water. The mustangs ate, drank and rested their weary legs.

A few days later, just as the sun was reaching the treetops, Lenny spotted a new two-legged in the distance. This one was smaller than the ones Lenny had seen before. She quietly approached Lenny's pen, then stopped and gazed at Lenny with gentle curiosity.

Lenny was fearful of her, as Lenny was fearful of all two- leggeds. Her instincts told her to fear all that are not herd-mates, but she could not help but feel the energy that surrounded this two-legged. It was sincere and it was good.

The next day, Lenny was sent into yet another box. This time the new two-legged, who said her name was Mary, peered through the cracks.

Lenny knew that her life was changing. She was afraid, but she reminded herself to have Faith. She was on her path - the one meant for her hooves only.

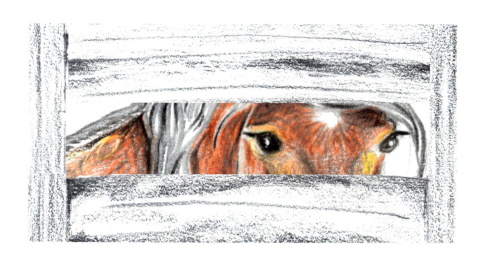

VII. A New Language

O̶nce in North Carolina, Mary and Lenny spent much time together. They were learning to communicate with one another. Lenny's language was not verbal like Mary's. Lenny's way of communicating was based on body movements, which was how she and her herdmates "spoke" to one another in the wild. Mary used her body movements in the same way Lenny did. Lenny liked that. This way they spoke through body language comforted her.

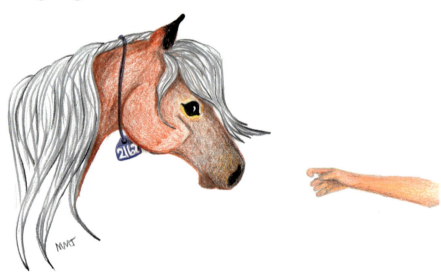

Lenny found she was picking up on Mary's two-legged language as well. She began to understand some of Mary's words and many of her tones. Lenny could understand if Mary wanted her to speed up, or stop, or just to relax - all by the sound of Mary's voice.

Mary and Lenny were gradually combining their languages and developing one of their own. Through this process, Mary was becoming Lenny's lead horse. Lenny took comfort in their new relationship.

There is nothing more important to a mustang than her lead horse.

Lenny was growing to respect Mary in the same way that her White Mountain herd had respected Queen, their lead mare and Lenny's mother. Lenny felt safe when Mary gave her direction and guidance. Oh, how Lenny loved to feel safe with Mary, her new herdmate, her new lead horse.

Mary and Lenny continued to develop their unique language and their relationship grew strong. It had been ninety days since Lenny first spotted Mary approaching her paddock and the big day of the challenge was quickly approaching.

Mary began to pack. Lenny watched Mary as she scurried about, putting things in the big box. Mary explained to Lenny that they were headed to Texas for the competition they had been practicing for.

Lenny could not fully understand what was going on, but she could feel Mary's excitement and that made her excited too. Lenny followed Mary into the big box and along with the rest of their family, they took off to Fort Worth, Texas.

VIII. The Mustang Competition

When Lenny and Mary arrived in Texas, they were thrilled to see so many other mustangs. They had each traveled from their new homes scattered all across the country to compete together.

The Mustang Heritage Foundation beamed with pride as they witnessed the mustangs' beauty and talent shine bright with their new two-legged partners. It was unimaginable to think that before this challenge was created, these mustangs were considered unwanted.

Mary and Lenny performed the patterns and navigated the obstacles. Lenny could feel that Mary was relaxed and confident. The unique language they had developed enabled Lenny to understand Mary's mind and thoughts. Lenny took comfort in Mary's security and they performed well together.

When the results were announced, they found that their confidence as a team had earned them a spot in the finals. They were to perform their freestyle before a live audience that very night!

The air was filled with excitement, as the two-leggeds anxiously waited to see the mustangs perform. Lenny and Mary listened to the roar of the crowd as they waited their turn.

Before long their names were announced, and they entered the arena. Lenny willingly stepped up on her pedestal as Mary asked. The crowd roared with excitement. Flashes could be seen from all around the large dome arena, as the two-leggeds snapped pictures and clapped their hands. Mary's heart raced faster and faster with each roar of the crowd.

Lenny felt Mary's heart race and she grew fearful. In the same way that she grew fearful in the wild when the leader of her herd became frightened. How Lenny wished Mary would exude the quiet confidence that she had before.

Lenny's heart raced faster and faster to match the rhythm of Mary's. Lenny needed Mary to tell her they would be safe, but all she felt from Mary was fear.

The performance was a blur, neither Mary nor Lenny relaxed until they finally exited the arena and the noise from the crowd subsided.

Lenny could feel Mary's disappointment and insecurity as they had to enter the arena for the awards presentation. The crowd began to roar as the winners were announced. Lenny danced in place, desperate for her lead horse, Mary, to help. Mary usually gave Lenny such security, but not now. It was as if Mary was not even there. She was simply sitting on Lenny's back. Nothing more than a passenger. Lenny felt so alone and afraid.

In that very moment, just when Lenny felt she could not handle the fear any longer, the mustang beside her quietly moved to put himself between Lenny and the crowd. His name was Murray and he knew without asking that his calm presence would give Lenny comfort. Lenny sighed in relief as she felt the blanket of security that Murray offered.

Murray softly said, "Those two-leggeds haven't a clue how scary they look from in here."

Lenny turned an ear to him in thankful response.

After the competition Lenny, Mary and their family traveled back to their North Carolina home. Lenny could feel Mary's sadness. It was as if Mary's disappointment in herself during the freestyle had stolen her Faith. Without Faith, Mary was blind to her special path. The path that Faith enabled her heart to see.

Lenny knew how Mary felt. She remembered when she lost her own path. She had felt no one wanted to give her a forever home because she was too old. The other mustangs had made her feel even worse by criticizing her silver mane. It hurt Lenny to think of Mary feeling this way.

Lenny wanted to tell Mary that she must have Faith. She must have Faith that there was something more powerful than her that had her best interest at heart.

Lenny remembered the kind words of Mikey the mustang. His simple compliment had given her the strength to remember her mother's wisdom about Faith. Oh, how Lenny wished Mary would experience something like that, something to help Mary find her own Faith once again.

IX. New Adventures

*M*ary came skipping over to Lenny's pasture. She had an extra jump in her step that excited Lenny. Mary said she had found a new adventure for them, so back into the box and down the road they went. They were off to a trail ride sponsored by The American Competitive Trail Horse Association (ACTHA) - an association that creates trail rides where horse and rider teams are judged as they navigate obstacles along the trail.

Neither Lenny nor Mary knew it yet, but this simple trail ride competition would give Mary the inspiration to find her Faith again. In the same way Mikey's words had given inspiration to Lenny, this trail competition gave inspiration to Mary.

Lenny and Mary had a blast. Lenny loved the freedom the trail offered her. It reminded Lenny of her days out in the wild, roaming free with her herd. The difference was that Mary was now Lenny's herdmate as well as her lead horse. Lenny found security in Mary just as she had found in her herd from White Mountain. Lenny knew this was what C.H. had meant when he told her of a forever home.

Lenny's wish had been granted. Mary's Faith was growing stronger with every stride, on this path they traveled together.

It had been exactly a year since they first met when Mary told Lenny they were headed for yet another adventure. It turned out that one of their ACTHA excursions had been an audition and they had been selected to appear on a television series called "America's Favorite Trail Horse."

Out of over one thousand auditions, they were among only one hundred finalists chosen to travel to Texas for the filming. They would share their partnership with the world on the television series and it would be up to the viewers to pick the winner.

Lenny watched as Mary began to pack the horse trailer once again and then it was time for Lenny, Mary and their family to head back to Texas!

X. New Friends

*M*ary and Lenny traveled to the beautiful hill country of Blanco, Texas. The rocks and hills reminded Lenny of her White Mountain homeland. Her mustang hooves were strong and she felt right at home crossing the slick rock bridges to navigate the trail.

Each of the horse and rider teams were filmed as celebrity judges critiqued them navigating obstacles out along the trail. The teams were not allowed to practice beforehand. In filming the first approach, the producers were able to show the relationship and trust of each team in an unfamiliar situation.

Lenny met all kinds of interesting horses while filming. One kind mare, named Blue, accompanied Lenny for a while. Blue was from Ohio and had grown up with an Amish family whose young children would ride her to gather their milk cows every morning. Blue told Lenny that she had traveled to Texas with her new partner, Kathy. Lenny had seen Blue jump the log and it was obvious she was confident in her relationship with Kathy.

It comforted Lenny to see other horses with such strong bonds with their two-leggeds - this America's Favorite Trail Horse setting felt like it was a good place to be.

Lenny met many other interesting teams. She was really excited when she met Shine, a beautiful golden dun. Shine was an American Mustang too! She was gathered from a mustang herd in Utah, just like Lenny was gathered from her Wyoming herd.

Shine had a wonderful relationship with her two-legged, named Lorrie. Lenny remembered seeing Shine in the finals of the mustang competition that she and Mary were in. The Mustang Heritage Foundation really had helped so many un-wanted mustangs find forever homes. How wonderful it was to see other mus-tangs that had such strong partnerships with their two-leggeds.

Lenny shared her barn with Lacie, a beautiful, dapple grey, American Quarter Horse. Lacie and her two-legged partner, Amanda, were both young and adventurous. Every night Lenny listened as Amanda sung to Lacie. They would even create songs together - they really did! Amanda would sing and Lacie would move the guitar strings with her muzzle. Lenny loved to see how relaxed Lacie was with Amanda close by.

The bond that each horse had with their two-legged human partner comforted Lenny. The energy she felt all around was pure, kind and sincere.

XI. Faith in One Another

Finally, it was time for Mary and Lenny to have their time in front of the cameras. Lenny bravely crossed each obstacle for Mary. She jumped the log with room to spare. She carefully crossed the slick rock bridge. She backed up the steep hill without hesitation. With every obstacle they crossed, their Faith in one another grew stronger.

Then came the ultimate test of trust and of Faith. They began to descend down a steep, narrow path that led to a deep river. The water was dark at the bottom of the path and resembled a bottomless hole. Lenny grew tense as Mary urged her forward. Her mustang instincts told her that the dark hole meant danger and that she must turn around and flee!

Mary felt Lenny's heart begin to race and she knew it was her duty as lead horse to give Lenny security and guidance. Mary knew Lenny's heart and thoughts would mirror hers. With that in mind, Mary took a deep breath, then very slowly let it out. As Mary exhaled, they both could feel all negative emotions vanish from their bodies.

Mary softly closed her legs on Lenny's sides to guide her onward. Lenny's instincts still screamed at her, "Turn around and Flee!" However, her instincts also reminded her that Mary was her lead horse and that her lead horse would keep her safe. So, with the security of Mary's gentle guidance, Lenny continued down the steep path.

Lenny's heartbeat gradually relaxed and slowed to match the rhythm of Mary's. Lenny was confident in Mary as lead horse and she was thankful Mary was offering her calm, confident guidance.

The cool water crept up Lenny's legs as she descended into the dark hole. The water slowly worked its way up to her belly as they walked deeper into the river. The cool water felt so good. Lenny let out a deep sigh of relief as she thought to herself that Mary had been right, they would be safe, safe together.

Lenny drug her muzzle across the water and took long, deep drinks as they slowly walked through the cool river. Lenny thought about how safe she felt with Mary there to guide her. Lenny thought about how happy she was to have her forever home and how she would not have found it without remembering her mother's words - *Have Faith Lenny, have Faith.*

In the same moment Mary was running her fingers through Lenny's silver mane. She thought of how she adored Lenny's unique mane and how this felt so right, this path, this mustang, this Faith.

As they quietly walked through the river, their hearts softly beat in rhythm together. They never noticed the cameras filming or the famous judges critiquing.

None of that mattered, for they had found their special path. Their Faith had opened the eyes of their hearts and they now could clearly see the path laid out before them.

Along this journey of Faith, they had found a forever home
                              - in one another.

Epilogue

I am honored that you have taken the time to read about our journey. Our story, portrayed in this book, is based on the true life adventures of myself and my special American Mustang partner, Lindsay's Faith. (known as "Lenny" in the book.) In the story, Lenny's thoughts are humanized a bit, in hopes of better relating with each of you!

Lindsay's Faith did, in fact, grow up in the wild of White Mountain, Wyoming. She had multiple babies in the wild before being gathered by the BLM, at which time, she was in foal yet again. She turned six years old while living at a BLM holding facility. This equates to a person in their thirties! She was deemed "un-adoptable" due to her age and entered in the Supreme Extreme Mustang Makeover. This was the mustang competition created by the Mustang Heritage Foundation, targeted at helping unwanted mustangs find forever homes. I adopted her via an auction aired on TV for $800. I can not express how excited I was to meet her and how much meeting her has changed my life!

We picked Lindsay's Faith up May of 2010 and I had 100 days to gentle and train her for the Supreme Extreme Mustang Makeover, to be held August 2010. As the story tells, we did not win that competition, but our journey of faith had just begun.

Lindsay's Faith & Mary
~ First Touch

The TV show, America's Favorite Trail Horse, was filmed one year after the day I met Lindsay's Faith for the first time. It was aired in the Fall of 2011. Voters from all over the country awarded Lindsay's Faith the winner of America's Favorite Trail Horse. With that title came $30,000 and along the journey to it - came the inspiration for this book.

I truly believe that we all deserve to have faith in ourselves, as well as faith that there is a power out there with our best interest at heart. I feel like, without faith, we are like mice in a complex maze. When we rely on only our physical eyes to see, we are limited to what is directly in front of us. We could spend ten lifetimes aimlessly scurrying about, trying to find our path to the finish line and still never find it. Yet, if we allow ourselves to have faith, therefore tuning in to the eyes of our heart, we are able to be led down our correct path in this complex maze of life.

It's as if the eyes of the heart can see glimpses of that maze from above - guiding us correctly through each winding turn.

If this story reaches out to even one child, or adult, I will feel it was worth writing. We are ALL unique, special and perfect in our own ways. It is sad that, like Lenny's silver mane, the qualities that make us special can be the same qualities of which we feel ashamed.

It is easy to make yourself feel superior by criticizing someone else for being different from you. I feel that as life goes on, it is those that hold on to their unique qualities that will be truly happy. Those individuals who remain true to themselves and follow the eyes of their heart - those are the ones I look up to and admire.

So, hold fast to what makes you - well, YOU.

For me it has always been horses. They have given me confidence and self worth through every phase of my life I have yet to experience. Horses have been a true gift to me and I owe everything that I am to them.

In addition to holding fast to what makes us unique, I feel we have a duty to lift the spirits of those around us. Words have such power. I feel that when we have a positive thought enter our mind regarding another being, we have a duty to express it out loud. Just as Mikey did for Lenny when he complimented her silver mane. We should also realize that bullies use the power of negative words, only to make themselves feel superior. It is compensation for their own lack of self worth and lack of confidence, but as powerful as negative words can be, we still have the strength to rise above them by focusing our thoughts on something positive.

Everyone has something unique that they have a right to be proud of. You might not know what it is yet, but there is no doubt that you have it within you. Have faith that you are special and before long you will see what it is that makes you special.

Mary and Lindsay's Faith - with Filleigh Kay on the way.

Faith allows the eyes of the heart to see.

~ Mary Miller-Jordan

Sites of Interest

American Competitive Trail Horse Association (ACTHA) ~ A national association that creates organized competitive trail rides. (They also created the TV show **America's Favorite Trail Horse** that Lenny and Mary won.) To find an ACTHA ride near you please visit www.actha.us

Bureau of Land Management (BLM) ~ The US Government management of public lands and management of the wild mustangs that call these lands home. For more information visit www.blm.gov

High Cotton Horse Farm ~ Where Lindsay's Faith, Mike, Mary and Filleigh Kay reside along with 14 other horses, 5 dogs, two cats and a pot-bellied pig. Visit www.highcottonhorsefarm.com to follow future mustang adventures!

Mustang Heritage Foundation (MHF) ~ A 501 (c)(3) public, charitable, nonprofit organization dedicated to facilitating successful adoptions for America's excess mustangs. Program areas focus on adopters, philanthropists, youth and horse training professionals. To participate in an Extreme Mustang Makeover, or to adopt a gentled wild horse, or to help monetarily fund this wonderful organization please visit www.mustangheritagefoundation.org

Rider4Helmets ~ An international campaign designed to encourage all riders to wear safety helmets ~ After the inspiration of her daughter's birth, Mary ALWAYS wears a helmet when she rides and she is very adamant about encouraging others to do so as well. For valuable information on helmet safety and more please visit www.riders4helmets.com

Made in the USA
San Bernardino, CA
16 August 2016